THE BOOK A ... THAT WORK TOGETHER

ANCIENT GREECE

TWO CAN

Created and published by
Two-Can Publishing Ltd
346 Old Street
London
EC1V 9NQ

Disk
Creative Director: William Wharfe
Programming Director: Paul Steven
Art Director: Sarah Evans
Designer: James Evans
Editor: Lyndall Thomas
Programmer: Craig Grummitt
Consultant: Dr Emma Dench
Illustrators: Michele Egar, Carlo Tartaglia, Jon Stuart
Production Director: Lorraine Estelle
Production Controller: Katherine Harvey
Project Manager: Joya Bart-Plange

Book
Creative Director: William Wharfe
Editor: Lyndall Thomas
Author: Robert Nicholson
Designer: Michele Egar
Consultant: Dr Emma Dench
Production Director: Lorraine Estelle
Production Controller: Katherine Harvey
Project Manager: Joya Bart-Plange

MAC ISBN 1-85434-625-3
PC ISBN 1-85434-624-5
CD ISBN 1-85434-626-1

Dewey Decimal Classification 938

2 4 6 8 10 9 7 5 3 1

A catalogue record for this book is available from the British Library

Printed in Hong Kong by Wing King Tong

Photographic Credits: Front cover: AKG Photo
Ancient Art and Architecture Collection: p13 (r), p14, p15 (b), p20, p23 (t);
Bridgeman Art Library: p26 (r), p27 (b); ET Archive: p17, p34 (l); Werner Forman: pp10-11;
Michael Holford: p13 (t,c), p15 (t), p19, p23 (b), p24 (t), p26 (l), p27 (t), p28, p34(tr), p46, p47;
Toby Maudsley: pp24-25 (b); Zefa: p34 (br)
Illustration Credits: Mike Allport: pp8-27, p47, p48; Maxine Hamil: pp29-33

INTERFACT

THE BOOK AND DISK THAT WORK TOGETHER

INTERFACT will have you hooked in minutes – and that's a fact!

The disk is packed with interactive activities, puzzles, quizzes and games that are great fun to do and full of interesting facts.

Put your knowledge of the ancient Greeks to the test in a challenging quiz!

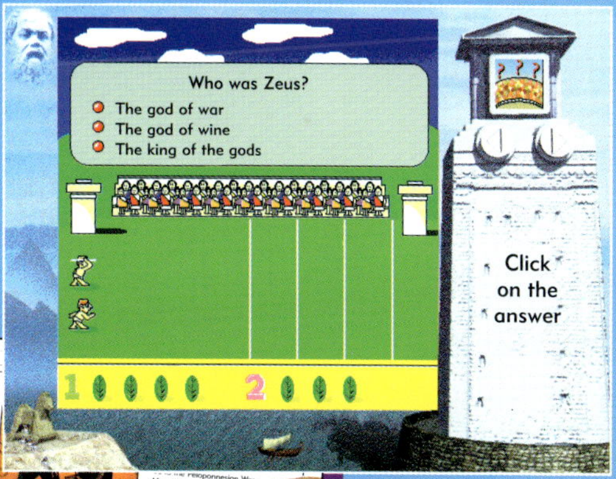

Open the book and discover more fascinating information highlighted with lots of full-colour illustrations and photographs.

Read up all about the peoples of ancient Greece and the cities they lived in.

To get the most out of **INTERFACT**, use the book and disk together. Look out for the special signs, called Disk Links and Bookmarks. To find out more, turn to page 43.

BOOKMARK

DISK LINK
Need some advice about life in ancient Greece? Then ask AT THE ORACLE!

Once you've clicked on to **INTERFACT**, you'll never look back.

LOAD UP!
Go to page 40 to find out how to load your disk and click into action.

What's on the disk

HELP SCREEN

Learn how to use the disk in no time at all.

Get to grips with the controls and find out how to use:

- arrow keys
- reading boxes
- 'hot' words

THE HIGH CITY

Here's your chance to visit the ancient city of Athens!

Spend some time at the Acropolis. You'll discover the Parthenon and you may even meet a god or two! Then, visit the agora to find out all about the ancient Greek way of life.

PAST-TIMES

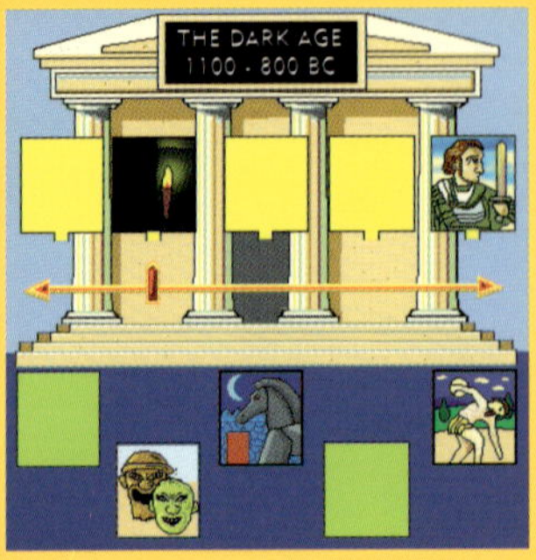

Let Plato and Aristotle take you on an exciting journey through time!

These great thinkers will give you the lowdown on Greece – from the early days to modern times. Learn how past events have helped to shape our world.

AT THE ORACLE

Are you full of questions about the ancient Greeks?

Then why not ask the Pythia? This famous priestess has all the answers you'll ever need. Visit the oracle at Delphi and pop some questions.

THE WRITE STUFF

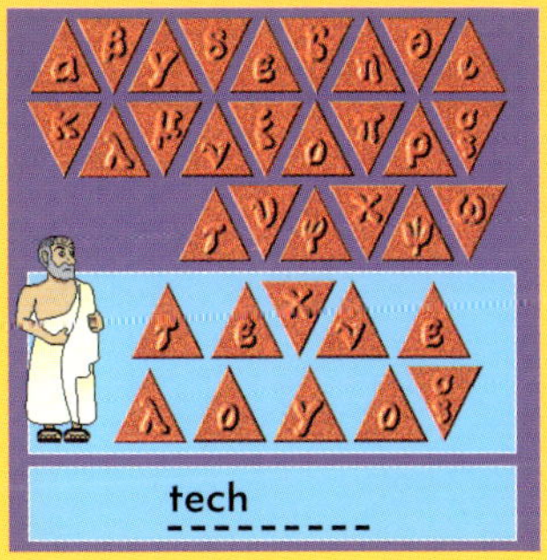

Take a good look at the letters of the Greek alphabet.

You'll find that Aristotle has got what it takes to guide you through the Greek language. He's got an epic story to tell – and he'll give you a few pointers on English as well!

ANCIENT ODYSSEY

Go on an interactive adventure in ancient Greece!

Are you feeling heroic? Then get set to take part in this exciting adventure game! You'll meet Odysseus, an ancient hero, and together you'll go on a journey to remember!

OLYMPIC CHALLENGE

Are you a champion when it comes to ancient Greece?

Take part in this challenging quiz. Every correct answer will help you to compete in the javelin event. So, the more you know, the further you'll throw!

THE STATE OF THINGS

Have a go at putting the city states in their place!

The Greek territories are in a bit of a state. If you can put things in order, you'll learn about the battles that the gruesome Greeks got themselves into.

What's in the book

*All words in the text that appear in **bold** can be found in the glossary*

The Greek world

The civilisation of ancient Greece began around 2000 BC. The Greeks controlled the mainland and the islands we now know as Greece. As the civilisation expanded, traders and farmers settled in the lands at the eastern end of the Mediterranean Sea.

The peak of the Greek civilisation was known as the Classical period, between 479 BC and 323 BC. During this time, the Greeks developed many new ideas about science and the arts. Some of their ideas and inventions influenced other civilisations in Europe. From there, Greek ideas spread all around the world.

DISK LINK
Travel in the lands of ancient Greece when you take part in the ANCIENT ODYSSEY.

Land and climate

Mainland Greece and the nearby islands are hot and dry, with high mountains and steep-sided valleys. The mainland is surrounded almost entirely by water. It was once covered in forest but, by the Classical period, many trees had been cut down. The scarce farmland was mainly near the coast, or in sheltered valleys. The most important crops were wheat, barley, grapes and olives. The Greeks were skilled sailors and keen traders, and they imported a lot of their food. There were few good roads and most journeys had to be made on foot. Some of the village communities were very isolated.

▼ As travelling overland was so difficult, the Greeks often travelled by sea. They found their way by staying close to the coasts. The sea was often stormy and sometimes there were attacks by pirates.

▶ This picture shows some olive trees growing on a dry, rocky hillside.

DISK LINK
Want to know more about how the land lies? Then take a look at THE STATE OF THINGS.

The city states

Greece was not always a united country as it is today. It was once made up of separate city states. Each city state was based around one city and included the surrounding farms and villages.

Athens was one of the largest and most powerful city states. At the height of the Classical period, there were more than 250,000 people living in the city and the surrounding countryside. Artists, philosophers and politicians from Athens were famous throughout Greece.

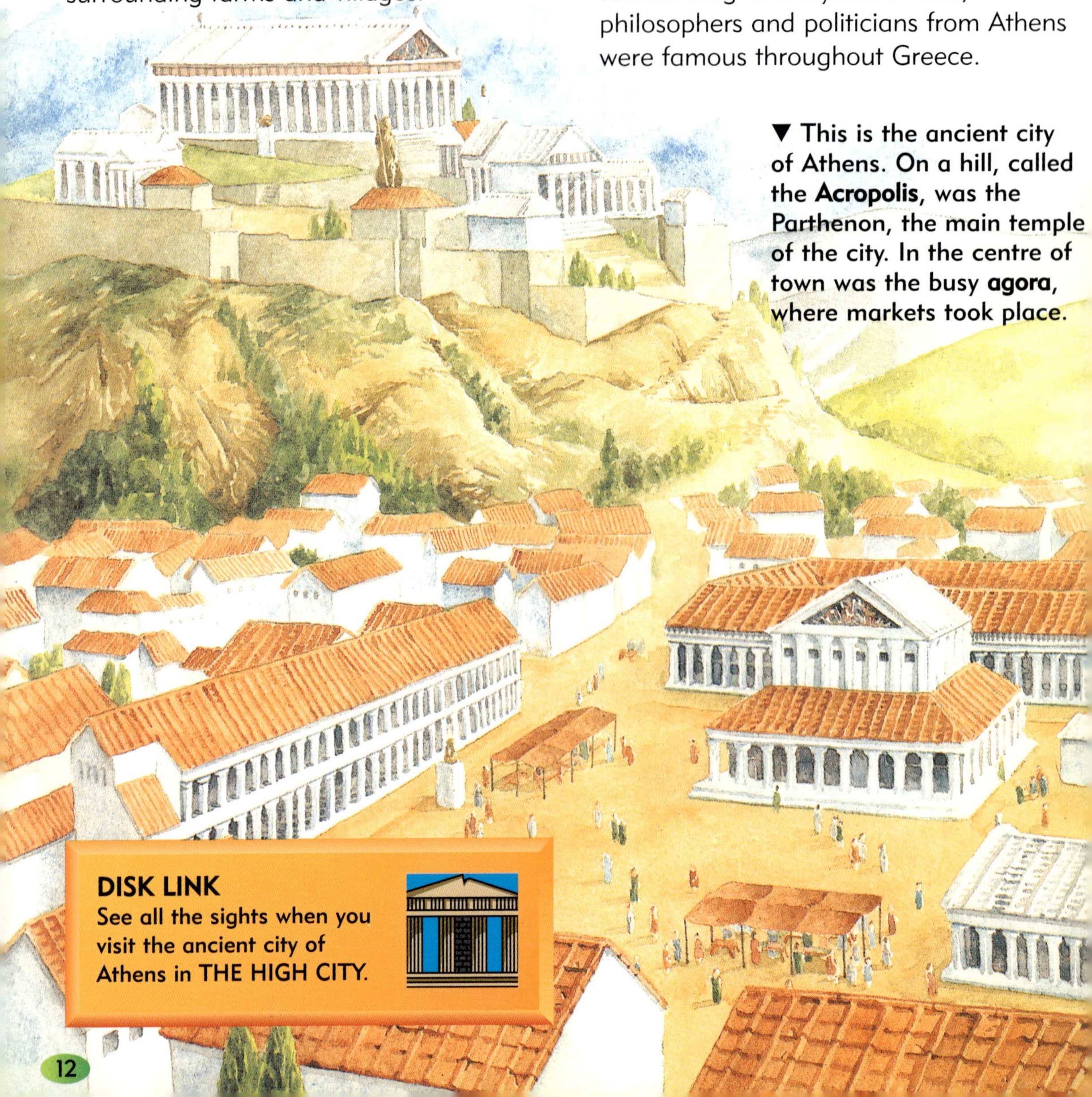

▼ This is the ancient city of Athens. On a hill, called the **Acropolis**, was the Parthenon, the main temple of the city. In the centre of town was the busy **agora**, where markets took place.

DISK LINK
See all the sights when you visit the ancient city of Athens in THE HIGH CITY.

Athens vs Sparta

Sparta was Athens' main rival. There were many wars between the two cities as they both tried to gain control of the whole of Greece. Sparta was famed for the strength of its army. In 431 BC, the rivalry between the two cities led to the Peloponnesian War. After 27 years of fighting, Sparta won the war.

▲ This vase painting shows some Greek soldiers in battle.

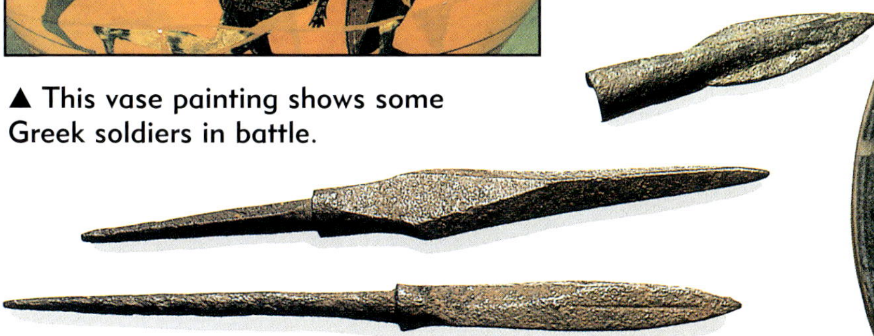

▲ Ancient Greek soldiers used weapons and armour made from iron or bronze.

Citizens and slaves

In ancient Greece, some groups of people had different rights from others. **Citizens** were the most important group of people and they had the most rights. They could own property and take part in politics. Only adult men were allowed to be citizens in ancient Greece.

Slaves were the property of their owners and they had no rights at all. Many slaves lived in miserable conditions. But some slaves were paid for the work that they did and, if they saved enough money, they could buy their freedom.

▲ **These are some ancient Greek coins.**

▼ **Soldiers often watched over slaves as they worked.**

DISK LINK
Read these pages very carefully! You might find some clues that will help you in the OLYMPIC CHALLENGE!

Government

In many of the city states in ancient Greece, the government was run as a **democracy**. All of the decisions about the city state were made by councils of citizens. Other city states, however, were ruled by rich and powerful landowners.

In Athens, all citizens could vote to decide on issues such as the type of taxes to be paid and whether or not to go to war. All citizens could take part in politics and legal affairs. Some citizens were paid a full day's wages to attend the government assemblies.

▲ This vase painting shows some women collecting water. Women didn't have the same rights as men in ancient Greece.

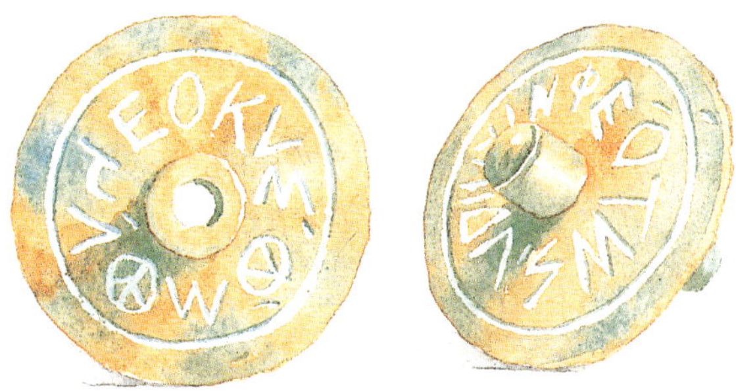

▲ Discs such as these were used to vote in courts of law. Hollow discs stood for 'guilty' and solid discs stood for 'not guilty'.

▲ Citizens could vote against a politician by writing his name on a pottery fragment, called an ostrakon.

Philosophy and science

The ancient Greeks were curious about themselves and the world around them. They made many important advances in science, learning and the arts. Great thinkers were known as **philosophers**, no matter what subject they studied. The word philosopher comes from the Greek words for 'lover of wisdom'. Philosophers tried to find out how the universe worked and how people should best live their lives.

Many Greek discoveries provide the foundations of our knowledge and beliefs. The Greeks studied the stars and learned that the Earth floats freely in space and turns on an imaginary line, called an axis. They also correctly predicted eclipses of th Sun. But sometimes the Greeks were wron One scholar, called Ptolemy, thought that the Earth was the centre of the universe.

Few of the Greeks' ideas were used for solving practical problems. For example, they did not use their metal-working techniques to make tools that would increase their knowledge of science.

Famous philosophers

● **Socrates** (about 469 - 399 BC)
Socrates was one of the first great philosophers of Classical Greece. He questioned many of the beliefs of the time.

● **Hippocrates** (about 469 - 399 BC)
Hippocrates was alive at the same time as Socrates. He practised scientific medicine and studied the human body.

● **Plato** (about 429 - 347 BC)
Plato founded a school in Athens, called The Academy, where he taught Aristotle.

● **Aristotle** (about 384 - 322 BC)
Aristotle examined things in nature and developed a way of thinking called **logic**.

▲ A bust of Socrates.

◀ The philosopher Eratosthenes used the Sun to calculate the circumference of the Earth. At noon, the Sun was directly overhead in Syene, in Southern Egypt. So, he measured the angle of the Sun at Alexandria, in Northern Egypt and then measured the distance between the two places. His calculation of the Earth's circumference was out by just 320 km.

DISK LINK
Would you like to meet some great thinkers? Then take a look at PAST-TIMES.

Gods and goddesses

The Greeks worshipped many gods and goddesses that represented parts of human life or the natural world. The gods were thought to live on **Mount Olympus** and there were many stories about them, in which they fought amongst each other or fell in love, just like men and women.

There were many temples where priests or priestesses performed rituals in honour of the gods. Offerings of food and wine were made and, sometimes during festivals, **sacrifices** were made.

The Greeks believed that the gods controlled events. So, they looked to the gods for answers to their problems. Some problems were solved by a **soothsayer**, who studied the weather, or the remains of animals, for answers from the gods. Other problems required a visit to an **oracle**, where a priest or priestess passed on messages from the gods.

▼ At the oracle in Delphi, a priestess, called the Pythia, went into a trance to receive messages from the gods.

The Olympic Games

In ancient Greece, games and festivals were held to honour the gods. The Olympic Games were held in Olympia in honour of Zeus every four years. They lasted for five days, and the events included boxing, wrestling, running, long-jump, discus-throwing, javelin-throwing and chariot races. People came from all over Greece to compete in the games. All wars were postponed so that people could travel safely to see them.

Important gods

ZEUS was the king of the gods.
HERA was married to Zeus. She was the queen of the gods.
POSEIDON was the god of the sea.
DIONYSUS was the god of wine.
ARES was the god of war.
HERMES was the messenger of the gods.
APOLLO was the god of music and healing.

▲ Aphrodite, the goddess of love.

◀ Athena, the goddess of wisdom, was born from the head of Zeus.

Theatre and writing

The Greeks were one of the first groups of people to record their history as it happened. Before this, people had passed on information by word of mouth. Poetry was the earliest form of Greek literature. Many of the poems told stories about heroes and gods. Homer was an ancient storyteller. He composed two **epic** poems, called the *Iliad* and the *Odyssey*. These and many other examples of Greek literature have survived until today.

▲ The actors in comedies wore padded costumes to make them look funny.

Drama

Drama developed from songs and dances that honoured the gods. Plays were an important part of religious festivals and many of the theatres were built next to temples. There were two sorts of plays: tragedies and comedies. Tragedies were sad tales about gods, heroes and legendary people. Comedies made fun of politics, religion and important people.

Greek actors always wore masks that showed different moods and expressions. The masks had wide mouths so that the actors' voices could be heard.

DISK LINK
Is Greek a lot like English? You'll find out if you've got THE WRITE STUFF!

At home

In ancient Greece, ordinary people lived in simple houses that were made from mud bricks. It was so easy to dig through the walls that burglars were known as wall-diggers! Each house was arranged around a courtyard, with an altar in the middle. The living rooms were on the ground floor, with bedrooms above.

Men and women often had separate living areas and spent most of their time apart. There were open fires in the kitchen and smoke escaped through a hole in the roof.

▼ This is the inside of a typical ancient Greek house.

:lothes

ʌen in ancient Greece wore tunics made rom wool or linen. Over this, they wore a ;quare piece of material, called a **chiton**, astened at the shoulders and belted at he waist. In colder weather, men wore a :loak, called a **himation,** draped around hem. In Classical times, it was very ashionable for men to have beards.

Women wore a long tunic, called a **peplos**. Wealthy people wore tunics made from decorated material, while slaves had plain tunics. Shoes were leather sandals or boots but many people went barefoot.

▼ A gold necklace of the sort worn by the woman in the vase painting (bottom).

▶ This vase painting shows a woman getting ready for her wedding. She is wearing a peplos.

◀ Some houses had a statue of the god ⅂ermes, called a herm, to guard the house.

Food

The ancient Greeks had a simple and healthy diet. They ate bread, cheese, fruit, vegetables, eggs and meat. Many Greeks lived near the sea, so fish and seafood were popular. Olive oil was used for cooking, lighting and cleaning.

The main meal was in the evening and the Greeks often held big dinner parties. They sat on couches, eating several courses and drinking lots of wine. After the meal, there was entertainment for the men at a **symposium**, or drinking party.

▲ This vase painting shows a messenger of the gods bringing a gift of grain.

DISK LINK
Keep your eyes peeled for information to help you in the OLYMPIC CHALLENGE!

▼ These are some examples of fruits that the ancient Greeks liked to eat.

Greek sweetmeats

Between courses at a dinner party, the Greeks ate sweetmeats – small snacks made from dates, figs, nuts, sesame seeds and honey. Here are some for you to make.

Put 100 g of sesame seeds into a saucepan with 4 large tablespoons of honey. Ask an adult to help you simmer the mixture over a low heat for 10-20 minutes, until it is a rich, golden colour. You can tell if it is ready by dropping a spoonful on to a wet plate, letting it cool, then working it into a ball. If it keeps its shape, it is ready. Take the pan off the heat and stir the mixture every few minutes until it is almost cold. Wet your hands with cold water and roll spoonfuls of the mixture into 20-25 little balls. Wrap each sweetmeat in greaseproof paper.

grapes

Arts and crafts

The Greeks thought that there was a perfect shape for every object, whether it was a simple clay pot or a huge temple. They used mathematics to try to make their art as beautiful as possible.

▲ The Greeks made elegant pots covered in patterns and paintings. Most of the pots were used every day, for storing water, oil, or wine. Some of the most beautiful pots were buried with the dead.

◀ This statue is made from stone. The Greeks were skilled sculptors and they made many statues from stone or bronze. The statues were detailed and lifelike, with expressive faces and clothes that looked real. Many of them were painted but have lost their colour over time.

▶ This is the Parthenon, in Athens. It is one of the inest examples of ancient Greek architecture that is still standing today. It was made from carved blocks of cream-coloured marble, held together with wooden pegs and metal clamps. The rows of columns are typical of ancient Greek buildings. This Classical style has been copied all over the world.

Bronze statues

Bronze statues were made using the 'lost wax' method.

Firstly, a clay model was made and wooden pegs were used to hold it together. Then, the model was covered with a thin layer of wax. The details of the statue's face and clothes were sculpted onto the wax.

The model was then covered with clay and heated, so the wax melted and ran out. Molten bronze was poured in between the clay layers.

▼ When the clay was finally removed, a bronze statue was revealed.

Language and learning

In ancient Greece, most children went to school. Boys went to school from the age of seven until they were 15. Boys learned reading, writing and maths, as well as music, poetry and sport. Some girls learned reading, writing, gymnastics and music. Girls were also taught the skills that they would need to run a household.

In Sparta, boys were taught to be tough to prepare them for their life as soldiers. At the age of seven, they went to a strict school where they learned how to fight and use weapons. They often went hungry and had to sleep on the ground, and sometimes they were beaten.

▶ This ancient terracotta doll has jointed arms and legs.

◀ This is an ancient baby's bottle.

The Greek alphabet

Some Greek letters are similar to those we use today. You may have heard some of their names before. Can you think where our word 'alphabet' comes from?

Greek letter	Name	English sound									
Α α	alpha	a	Η η	eta	ey	Ν ν	nu	n	Τ τ	tau	t
Β β	beta	b	Θ θ	theta	th	Ξ ξ	xi	ks	Υ υ	upsilon	u
Γ γ	gamma	g	Ι ι	iota	i	Ο ο	omicron	o	Φ φ	phi	ph
Δ δ	delta	d	Κ κ	kappa	k	Π π	pi	p	Χ χ	chi	ch
Ε ε	epsilon	e	Λ λ	lambda	l	Ρ ρ	rho	r	Ψ ψ	psi	ps
Ζ ζ	zeta	z	Μ μ	mu	m	Σ σ,ς	sigma	s	Ω ω	omega	oh

The legend of the Minotaur

The ancient Greeks told myths about their gods and about the world around them. Myths often included real events from Greek history. This myth is about an early civilisation on the island of Crete, long before Athens was a powerful city state. It tells the story of Theseus, a heroic young man who overcame the Minotaur, a terrifying beast that was half-man and half-bull.

Athenians were afraid of the island of Crete and trembled at the mention of it. Every nine years, King Minos of Crete demanded a terrible tribute from the Athenians. Seven young men and seven young women were taken from Athens to be fed to the fearsome Minotaur. King Minos would send a ship with black sails to Athens when the tribute was due. A huge crowd would gather at the harbour, weeping and wailing as the ship sailed away towards Crete.

When the prisoners arrived in Crete, they were given fine clothes and made guests of honour at a huge banquet. They were offered the most delicious food available but they could hardly eat. Afterwards, they were shut in a luxurious room but few of them could sleep.

The next day, they were taken to some huge, wooden doors, carved with pictures of galloping bulls. From behind the doors came the loud sounds of bellowing and stamping. The prisoners were very afraid.

Then, a guard opened the doors and pushed a prisoner through. The small crowd of prisoners, guards and priestesses outside heard a blood-curdling scream. A priestess pointed at the next prisoner to be sent through. This went on until all the prisoners had met their fate. Afterwards, the Athenians rested easy for nine years, until it was time to make another tribute.

Nine years passed and the dreaded ship was sent to Athens again. Amongst the prisoners sent to Crete this time was a young man, named Theseus. Unlike all the other prisoners, he sat dry-eyed on the ship. He laughed and chatted as they prepared for the banquet, which cheered up the other prisoners. At the banquet, Theseus sat next to King Minos' daughter, Ariadne, who was charmed by his courage and his handsome looks.

Ariadne told Theseus that behind the doors there was an elaborate maze. The paths twisted and turned, confusing the eye and the mind. No one who had entered the maze had ever returned.

The Minotaur lived at the very heart of the maze. He knew all the twists, turns and blind alleys. If someone stumbled into the maze, the Minotaur could find him or her within moments.

Ariadne was determined to help Theseus. After the banquet, she crept into the sleeping chamber and called softly to him. All of Theseus' weapons had been taken away so Ariadne handed him a sword. Then she led the way to the great carved wooden doors of the maze.

"I will wait here for you," she said and handed Theseus a ball of thread.

"What is this for?" Theseus said, puzzled.

"As you walk through the maze, unwind this thread behind you. If you succeed, you can follow the thread back. The Minotaur will be asleep, so creep silently through the passages until you reach his lair. With surprise on your side, you may beat him," Ariadne said.

Theseus took the thread from Ariadne and pushed open the great door. He stepped inside and closed the door, trapping the end of the thread in it. Then, holding his sword in front of him, Theseus headed into the maze.

Theseus could hear the Minotaur snoring and headed towards the noise. But a few minutes later, he could no longer hear the snores. The path had doubled back, and he was further away from the centre than when he had started. Theseus picked up the thread and followed it back to the last place where he had chosen a path.

"If I take the path that seems to lead towards the Minotaur, I end up further away," he said to himself. "But perhaps if I choose the path which seems to lead away, I will get closer to him."

Theseus crept quietly along and soon found himself stumbling into the mouth of a dark cave. From inside, he heard a huge roar, followed by the sound of heavy footsteps. The Minotaur had woken up!

Theseus gasped and dropped his sword. The Minotaur was even more terrifying than he had imagined. It had the body of a huge man and the head of an angry bull. Just as the Minotaur leapt forward to grab him, Theseus picked up his sword and struck the Minotaur a terrible blow on the leg.

The Minotaur was in agony. He was not used to people fighting back – his victims were usually prisoners who did not resist. Theseus struck once more with his sword. The Minotaur lay dead at his feet!

Picking up the end of the thread, brave Theseus retraced his steps through the maze. Ariadne was waiting for him at the outer doors.

Theseus was proclaimed a hero by the people of Athens. They were overjoyed that Athens no longer had to pay such a terrible tribute to King Minos of Crete.

How we know

How do we know so much about the Greeks when they lived so long ago?

▲ The painting on this plate shows two Greek heroes fighting over the body of a soldier.

Evidence from the ground

The Greeks built many buildings and made many beautiful objects. Some of these were buried and archaeologists have been able to dig them up to learn from them. Pictures on pottery, for example, tell us about the way that people looked.

▲ This picture is from Roman times. It shows Alexander the Great, a famous Greek military leader, going into battle against the Persian Empire.

Evidence from books

The ancient Greeks were one of the first groups of people to keep written records. They wrote down all sorts of things, from history and philosophy, to lists of goods in stores. Many of these have survived until today. They give us important clues about the ancient Greek way of life.

Evidence from around us

Greek buildings that remain standing today give us evidence of how the ancient Greeks lived. And some Greek words have become part of other European languages – especially words connected with science such as 'psychology' and 'astronomy'.

▲ Theseus' temple still stands in Athens.

Glossary

Acropolis
The hill within the boundary of a city state that was used for defence. This is a Greek word, meaning 'high city'.

agora
An open area in the centre of ancient Greek cities where markets took place.

chiton
A garment Greek men wore fastened at the shoulders and belted around the waist.

citizen
In ancient Greece, a citizen was a man who had the right to own property and take part in politics and the law.

democracy
A political system where citizens can vote for their leaders and can influence decisions about the way their city or country is run.

epic
A long, traditional poem that tells a story about heroes or the gods.

himation
A type of cloak worn by Greek men.

logic
A method of thinking a problem through carefully to find a solution.

Mount Olympus
The mountain in Greece where the gods were thought to live.

myths
Traditional stories about gods or heroes.

oracle
A holy place where priests and priestesses asked the gods for advice.

ostrakon
A pottery fragment that citizens wrote on to vote against a politician.

peplos
A long tunic worn by women in ancient Greece.

philosopher
A person who studies the world around them. This word comes from the Greek words for 'lover of wisdom.'

sacrifice
An offering, usually of an animal, made to the gods, asking them to bring good fortune to people.

slave
A worker who was owned by a citizen and had no rights at all.

soothsayer
A person who could predict the future and tell fortunes.

symposium
A drinking party, attended by Greek men, where entertainment took place.

Work book

Photocopy this sheet and use it to make your own notes.

Work book

Photocopy this sheet and use it to make your own notes.

Loading your INTERFACT disk

INTERFACT is available on floppy disk and CD-ROM for both PCs with Windows and Apple Macs. Make sure you follow the correct instructions for the disk you have chosen and your type of computer. Before you begin, check the minimum specification (inside front cover).

CD-ROM INSTRUCTIONS

If you have a copy of INTERFACT on CD, you can run the program from the disk – you don't need to install it on your hard drive.

PC WITH WINDOWS 95

1. Put the disk in the CD drive
2. Open MY COMPUTER
3. Double click on the CD drive icon
4. Double click on the icon called GREECE

PC WITH WINDOWS 3.1 OR 3.11

1. Put the disk in the CD drive
2. Select RUN from the FILE menu in the PROGRAM MANAGER
3. Type **D:\GREECE** (Where D is the letter of your CD drive)
4. Press the RETURN key

APPLE MAC

1. Put the disk in the CD drive
2. Double click on the INTERFACT icon
3. Double click on the icon called GREECE

FLOPPY DISK INSTRUCTIONS

If you have a copy of INTERFACT on floppy disk you must install the program on to your computer's hard drive before you can run it.

PC WITH WINDOWS 3.1 OR 3.11

To install INTERFACT:

1. Put the disk in the floppy drive
2. Select RUN from the FILE menu in the PROGRAM MANAGER
3. Type **A:\INSTALL** (Where A is the letter of your floppy drive)
4. Click OK – unless you want to change the name of the INTERFACT directory

To run INTERFACT:

Once the program has installed, open the INTERFACT group in the PROGRAM MANAGER and double click on the icon called GREECE

PC WITH WINDOWS 95

To install INTERFACT:

1. Put the disk in the floppy drive
2. Select RUN from the START menu
3. Type **A:\INSTALL** (Where A is the letter of your floppy drive)
4. Click OK – unless you want to change the name of the INTERFACT directory

To run INTERFACT:

Once the program has installed, open the START menu and select PROGRAMS then select INTERFACT and click on the icon called GREECE

APPLE MAC

To install INTERFACT:

1. Put the disk in the floppy drive
2. Double click on the icon called INTERFACT INSTALLER
3. Click CONTINUE
4. Click INSTALL – unless you want to change the name of the INTERFACT folder

To run INTERFACT:

Once the program has installed, open the INTERFACT folder and double click on the icon called GREECE

How to use INTERFACT

INTERFACT is easy to use. First find out how to load the program (see page 40) then read these simple instructions and dive in!

You will find that there are lots of different features to explore. Use the controls on the right-hand side of the screen to select the one you want to play. You will see that the main area of the screen changes as you click on to different features.

For example, this is what your screen will look like when you play At the Oracle, where the Pythia will answer all your questions. Once you've selected a feature, click on the main screen to start playing.

Click here to select the feature you want to play.

Click on the arrow keys to scroll through the different features on the disk or find your way to the exit.

This is the reading box where instructions and directions appear explaining what to do. Go to page 4 to find out what's on the disk.

DISK LINKS

When you read the book, you'll come across Disk Links. These show you where to find activities on the disk that relate to the page you are reading. Use the arrow keys to find the icon on screen that matches the one in the Disk Link.

DISK LINK
Fancy taking a look around the Acropolis? You can when you visit THE HIGH CITY!

BOOKMARKS

As you play the features on the disk, you'll bump into Bookmarks. These show you where to look in he book for more information about the topic on screen. Just turn to the page of the book shown n the Bookmark.

WORK BOOK

On pages 36-39 you'll find note pages to photocopy and use again and again. Use them to write down your own discoveries as you go through the book and the disk.

HOT DISK TIPS

- After you have chosen the feature you want to play, remember to move the cursor from the icon to the main screen before clicking on the mouse again.

- If you don't know how to use one of the on-screen controls, simply touch it with your cursor. An explanation will pop up in the reading box!

- Keep a close eye on the cursor. When it changes from an arrow ➔ to a hand ☞ click your mouse and something will happen.

- Any words that appear on screen in blue and underlined are 'hot'. This means you can touch them with the cursor for more information.

- Explore the screen! There are secret hot spots and hidden surprises to find.

Troubleshooting

If you have a problem with the INTERFACT disk, you should find the solution here. You can also call the helpline on 0171 684 4050. The lines are open from 10am to 5pm, Monday to Friday, and calls are charge at normal rates. But remember to get permission from the person who pays the bill before you use the phone

QUICK FIXES Run through these general checkpoints before consulting COMMON PROBLEMS (see opposite page).

QUICK FIXES

PC WITH WINDOWS 3.1 OR 3.11

1 Check that you have the minimum specification: 386/33Mhz, VGA colour monitor, 4Mb of RAM.

2 Make sure you have typed in the correct instructions: a colon (:) not a semi-colon (;) and a back slash (\) not a forward slash (/). Also, do not put any spaces between letters or punctuation.

3 It is important that you do not have any other programs running. Before you start **INTERFACT**, hold down the Control key and press Escape. If you find that other programs are open, click on them with the mouse, then click the End Task key.

QUICK FIXES

PC WITH WINDOWS 95

1 Make sure you have typed in the correct instructions: a colon (:) not a semi-colon (;) and a back slash(\) not a forward slash (/). Also, do not put any spaces between letters or punctuation.

2 It is important that you do not have any other programs running. Before you start **INTERFACT**, look at the task bar. If you find that other programs are open, click on them with the right mouse button and select Close from the pop-up menu.

QUICK FIXES

APPLE MAC

1 Make sure that you have the minimum specification: 68020 processor, 640x480 colour display, system 7.0 (or a later version) and 4Mb of RAM.

2 It is important that you do not have any other programs running. Before you start **INTERFACT**, click on the application menu in the top right-hand corner. Select each of the open applications and select Quit from the File menu.

COMMON PROBLEMS

Symptom: Cannot load disk.
Problem: There is not enough space available on your hard disk.
Solution: Make more space available by deleting old applications and programs you don't use until 6Mb of free space is available.

Symptom: Disk will not run.
Problem: There is not enough memory available.
Solution: *Either* quit other applications and programs (see Quick Fixes) ***or*** increase your machine's RAM by adjusting the Virtual Memory.

Symptom: Graphics do not load or are of poor quality.
Problem: *Either* there is not enough memory available ***or*** you have the wrong display setting.
Solution: *Either* quit other applications and programs (see Quick Fixes) ***or*** make sure that your monitor control is set to 256 colours (MAC) or VGA (PC).

Symptom: There is no sound (PCs only).
Problem: Your sound card is not Soundblaster compatible.
Solution: Configure sound settings to make them Soundblaster compatible (see your sound card manual for more information).

Symptom: Your machine freezes.
Problem: There is not enough memory available.
Solution: *Either* quit other applications and programs (see Quick Fixes) ***or*** increase your machine's RAM by adjusting the Virtual Memory.

Symptom: Text does not fit neatly into boxes and 'hot' copy does not bring up extra information.
Problem: Standard fonts on your computer have been moved or deleted.
Solution: Re-install standard fonts. The PC version requires Arial; the Mac version requires Helvetica. See your computer manual for further information.

Index

A

B

C

D

E

F

G

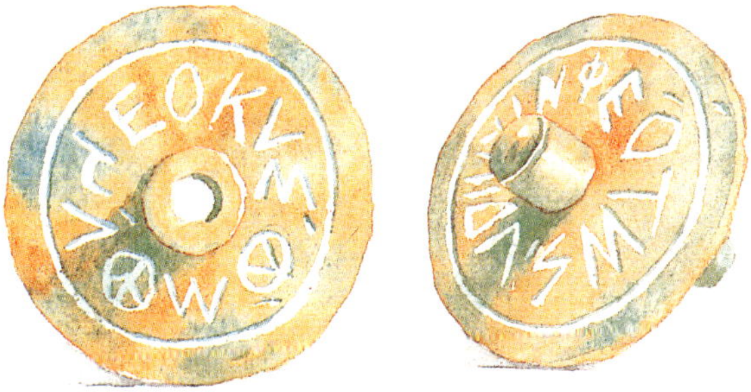